D0443979

EXPLORING SPACE

The Hubble Telescope

by Derek Zobel

Consultant:
Duane Quam, M.S. Physics
Chair, Minnesota State
Academic Science Standards
Writing Committee

BLASTOFF! READERS
3

BELLWETHER MEDIA • MINNEAPOLIS, MN

Note to Librarians, Teachers, and Parents:

Blastoff! Readers are carefully developed by literacy experts and combine standards-based content with developmentally appropriate text.

Level 1 provides the most support through repetition of high-frequency words, light text, predictable sentence patterns, and strong visual support.

Level 2 offers early readers a bit more challenge through varied simple sentences, increased text load, and less repetition of high-frequency words.

Level 3 advances early-fluent readers toward fluency through increased text and concept load, less reliance on visuals, longer sentences, and more literary language.

Level 4 builds reading stamina by providing more text per page, increased use of punctuation, greater variation in sentence patterns, and increasingly challenging vocabulary.

Level 5 encourages children to move from "learning to read" to "reading to learn" by providing even more text, varied writing styles, and less familiar topics.

Whichever book is right for your reader, Blastoff! Readers are the perfect books to build confidence and encourage a love of reading that will last a lifetime!

This edition first published in 2010 by Bellwether Media, Inc.

No part of this publication may be reproduced in whole or in part without written permission of the publisher. For information regarding permission, write to Bellwether Media, Inc., Attention: Permissions Department, 5357 Penn Avenue South, Minneapolis, MN 55419.

Library of Congress Cataloging-in-Publication Data

Zobel, Derek, 1983-
The Hubble Telescope / by Derek Zobel.
    p. cm. – (Blastoff! Readers. Exploring space)
Includes bibliographical references and index.
Summary: "Introductory text and full-color images explore the physical characteristics of the Hubble Telescope in space. Intended for students in kindergarten through third grade"–Provided by publisher.
ISBN 978-1-60014-296-3 (hardcover : alk. paper)
1. Hubble Space Telescope (Spacecraft)–Juvenile literature. 2. Orbiting astronomical observatories–Juvenile literature.
I. Title.
QB500.268.Z63 2010
522'.2919–dc22   2009037958

Text copyright © 2010 by Bellwether Media, Inc.
Printed in the United States of America, North Mankato, MN.
010110   1149

Contents

The Hubble Telescope is a **space telescope**. It is named after the **astronomer** Edwin Hubble.

Edwin Hubble

Astronomers use the Hubble
to look at objects in space.
It can take images to show
to people on Earth.

The Hubble launched in 1990.
A **space shuttle** carried it
into space.

The space shuttle put it in **orbit** above the **atmosphere**.

A team of **engineers** on the ground operates the telescope.

Telescopes on the ground can be blocked by clouds. The Hubble is above the clouds. It can see clearly into space.

solar arrays

The Hubble is powered by sunlight. Large **solar arrays** turn sunlight into electricity.

The solar arrays
are on the sides of
the telescope.

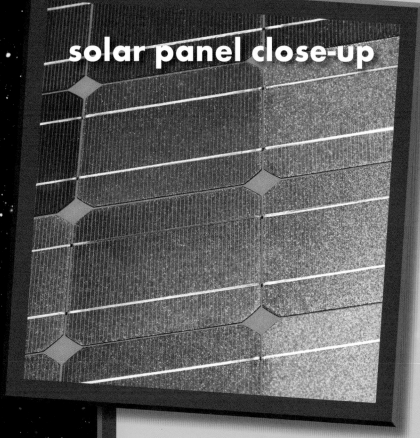

solar panel close-up

The Hubble uses light to look into space. The light enters through one end of the telescope.

The light reflects off of **mirrors**.
It is sent to several **instruments**.

mirrors

instruments

Some instruments search
for far-off planets that
circle other stars.

wide field image

One instrument can take images of large areas of space instead of just single objects. These are called "wide field" images.

One instrument senses heat. It can find places where stars are forming. It can also look deep into space.

The Hubble sends its images to **satellites** that orbit Earth.

The Hubble

satellite

The satellites then send the images down to the command center on the ground.

command center

The engineers and astronomers in the command center record the images. Astronomers from around the world can see the images.

Parts of the Hubble can break. **Astronauts** go up in a space shuttle to repair the telescope.

They make the Hubble work again so it can continue to show the wonders of space!

Glossary

astronauts—people who have been trained to fly aboard a spacecraft and work in space

astronomer—a scientist who studies space and objects in space

atmosphere—the gases around an object in space

engineers—people who plan and build machines

instruments—tools that scientists use; the Hubble has many instruments to see different objects in space.

mirrors—objects in some telescopes that reflect light so faraway objects can be seen

orbit—the path that an object takes when it circles the sun, a planet, or a moon

satellites—objects that are sent into space to orbit Earth; satellites can help predict weather, take pictures of Earth, or beam TV signals to Earth.

solar arrays—groups of solar panels that capture sunlight and turn it into electricity

space shuttle—a spacecraft that carries astronauts into space

space telescope—a telescope that takes images from above the atmosphere

To Learn More

AT THE LIBRARY

Carruthers, Margaret W. *The Hubble Space Telescope*. New York, N.Y.: Children's Press, 2004.

Cole, Michael D. *The Hubble Space Telescope*. Berkeley Heights, N.J.: Enslow Publishers, 1999.

Roza, Greg. *The Hubble Space Telescope: Understanding and Representing Numbers in the Billions*. New York, N.Y.: Powerkids Press, 2005.

ON THE WEB

Learning more about the Hubble Telescope is as easy as 1, 2, 3.

1. Go to www.factsurfer.com.

2. Enter "Hubble Telescope" into the search box.

3. Click the "Surf" button and you will see a list of related Web sites.

With factsurfer.com, finding more information is just a click away.

BLASTOFF! JIMMY CHALLENGE

Blastoff! Jimmy is hidden somewhere in this book. Can you find him? If you need help, you can find a hint at the bottom of page 24.

Index

Blastoff! Jimmy Challenge (from page 23).
Hint: Go to page 6 and blast off.